J616
Silverstein, Alvin
Tapeworms, foot fungus, lice, and
more :

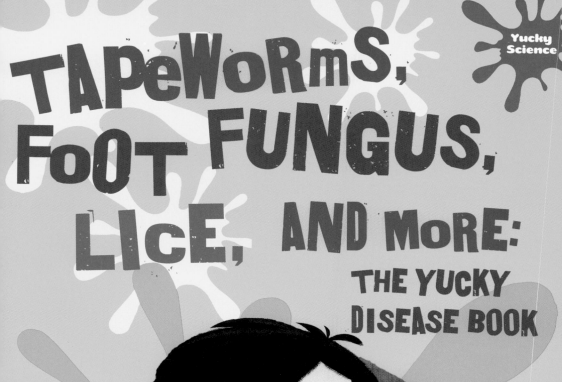

TAPEWORMS, FOOT FUNGUS, LICE, AND MORE:
THE YUCKY DISEASE BOOK

Yucky Science

Alvin and Virginia
Silverstein
and
Laura Silverstein Nunn

Illustrated by
Gerald Kelley

Library of Congress Cataloging-in-Publication Data:

Silverstein, Alvin.
    Tapeworms, foot fungus, lice, and more : the yucky disease book / by Alvin Silverstein,
Virginia Silverstein, and Laura Silverstein Nunn.
        p. cm. — (Yucky science)
    Summary: "Explores 'yucky' diseases, including leprosy, plague, tapeworms, and
more"—Provided by publisher.
    Includes bibliographical references and index.
    ISBN 978-0-7660-3314-6
    1. Medicine—Juvenile literature. 2. Diseases—Juvenile literature. I. Silverstein,
Virginia B. II. Nunn, Laura Silverstein. III. Title.
    R130.5.S533 2010
    616—dc22
                                                    2009012282

Printed in the United States of America

052010 Lake Book Manufacturing, Inc., Melrose, Prak, IL

10 9 8 7 6 5 4 3 2 1

To Our Readers: We have done our best to make sure all Internet Addresses in this book were
active and appropriate when we went to press. However, the author and the publisher have no
control over and assume no liability for the material available on those Internet sites or on other
Web sites they may link to. Any comments or suggestions can be sent by e-mail to comments@
enslow.com or to the address on the back cover.

♻ Enslow Publishers, Inc., is committed to printing our books on recycled paper. The paper
in every book contains 10% to 30% post-consumer waste (PCW). The cover board on the
outside of each book contains 100% PCW. Our goal is to do our part to help young people
and the environment too!

Illustration Credits: © 2009 Gerald Kelley, www.geraldkelley.com

Photo Credits: Andrew Syred/Photo Researchers, Inc., p. 22; Associated Press, p. 41;
© Barkley Fahnestock/iStockphoto.com, p. 28; CDC/Dr. Jack Poland, p. 9; courtesy of the
Abis family, Philippines, p. 8; Dr. Gary Gaugler/Visuals Unlimited, Inc., p. 14; Gustoimages /
Photo Researchers, Inc., p. 36; © James G. Mundie, p. 38; Mediscan/Visuals Unlimited, Inc.,
p. 34.

Cover Illustration: © 2009 Gerald Kelley, www.geraldkelley.com

Enslow Publishers, Inc.
40 Industrial Road
Box 398
Berkeley Heights, NJ 07922
USA

http://www.enslow.com

CONTENTS

What's Yucky?

Getting sick is no fun. When you have a cold, for example, your nose gets stopped up so you can't even breathe. Or it dribbles and runs, and you have to keep wiping it until it's red and raw. You cough and sneeze and spit out yucky, gooey globs of stuff. Your head hurts, and your throat is sore. You feel totally miserable. But after a week or so, that cold will just be a bad memory.

What about food poisoning? Maybe you ate some potato salad with mayo that sat out in the sun too long at a picnic. Or you made a sandwich with some old, leftover lunch meat. Now you're spending most of the day in the bathroom, throwing up and having diarrhea. Your stomach hurts, and just a few sips of water start you throwing up again.

Allergies are pretty yucky, too. Breathing air with dust or pollen that you can't even see may make you sneeze again and again. Eating certain foods or touching something like poison ivy can make you break out in an icky, itchy rash.

All those illnesses are yucky, but they're kind of ordinary. What about those really scary diseases that you may have seen on the news? Some rare ones actually make people bleed from their eyes, nose, and mouth, or waste away until they look like skeletons with skin. Some diseases are caused by tiny bugs. Does the idea of bugs or worms crawling under your skin give you the creeps?

Here's our pick of some of the world's yuckiest diseases.

CHAPTER ONE

Old-Time Diseases

"LEPER! KEEP AWAY!"

If you were living a few thousand years ago, you probably would have thought lepers were scary. Lepers are people who have leprosy, a disease that causes gross-looking skin rashes and open sores. Without treatment, the skin, muscles, and bones actually rot away! Leprosy can cause people to lose fingers, toes, or other body parts. In the past, many people were afraid to be around anyone with leprosy. They thought that touching lepers or even breathing the same air as lepers did could give them the disease, too.

Leprosy is caused by a bacterium (a kind of germ). It is spread by the coughs or sneezes of an

Yikes! In the Middle Ages, people were so afraid of getting leprosy that they sent lepers to leper colonies on faraway islands or in special hospitals. People even thought they could catch leprosy by handling money a leper had touched. So leper colonies used special tokens instead of regular money. Some leper colonies still exist! They are found in such places as Japan, India, Egypt, and Nepal.

This is real money that was used at a leper colony in the Philippines.

```
   I       This Certifies That The      I   I
!1¢!     PHILIPPINES  COMMONWEALTH     !1¢!
! __ !       BUREAU OF  HEALTH         !   !
1942       CULION LEPER COLONY          1942
       Is Obligated to  Pay the Bearer

       : : : : : :-ONE CENTAVO-: : : : : :

           In Legal  Tender Currency
Disb. Of?., C.I.C.    Adtg. Chief, C.L.C
       842          Chairman, E.C.C.    8424
```

infected person. But it is not as easy to catch as many people think. You can't get the disease by simply bumping into an infected person on the street. You would need to be with an infected person over a long period of time. Leprosy is more likely to spread in a family or a nursing home, for example.

People still get leprosy today. Fortunately, there are now medicines that can kill the germs and cure the disease.

BLACK DEATH

Another yucky old-time disease that is still around is the plague. The plague was a widespread killer disease in the Middle Ages. In the mid-1300s, it killed millions of people in Europe. In the twenty-first century, people sometimes still get the plague, but it is no longer so dangerous. Modern medicines can save people who get it.

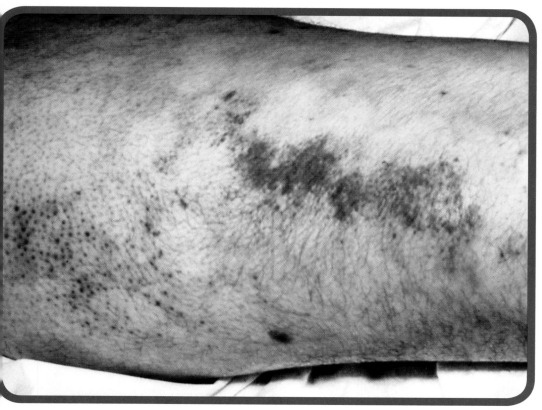

Bubonic plague causes infected people to break out in purplish black spots.

Yikes! During the Middle Ages, the plague killed 20 to 30 million people—about one-third of Europe's population at the time!

Why did they call the plague Black Death? One form of the disease made people break out in purplish black spots. They also developed swollen lymph glands. These glands contain disease-fighting cells. The swollen lymph glands were called buboes, which gave the disease one of its names: bubonic plague.

Another yucky thing about the plague is the way it spreads. Bubonic plague is caused by a bacterium. But people don't usually catch it directly from other people. First, the bacterium infects small rodents, such as rats, mice, or squirrels. The rodents may not get very sick, but they can carry plague bacteria in their blood and other body fluids. Fleas bite these animals and get infected, too. If the infected fleas bite people, they squirt bacteria into their skin. The people they bite can get *really* sick. During the Middle Ages, the Black Plague spread quickly because many homes and workplaces were overrun by huge numbers of flea-ridden rats.

CHAPTER TWO

Scary New Diseases

REAL-LIFE HORROR

Do you like scary movies? People who catch the Ebola virus may feel like they're living in a real-life horror movie. Their blood vessels may start to leak. Blood seeps out—through their mouth, eyes, and ears. Blood even leaks out of their organs and builds up inside the body. The person can literally bleed to death.

Ebola is a rare but deadly disease. Unlike the bubonic plague and leprosy, Ebola was not known about until fairly recently. It was discovered in 1976 in Africa. Most of the cases have occurred there. So far, there has not been a case of Ebola fever in the United States.

Yikes! People catch Ebola most often in hospitals. Some get it from infected blood when needles are reused for injections. Others catch it when Ebola patients cough or sneeze, or by touching things they have handled.

The illness starts suddenly, often within a few days after a person becomes infected. At first, it seems like a bad case of flu, with high fever, sore throat, headache, and body aches and pains. Then comes vomiting, diarrhea, and stomach pain. After a few days, the illness may get much worse. Some blood vessels begin to burst, spilling out blood. At this point, nothing can save the patient. There is no cure for Ebola, and no vaccine to prevent it.

FLESH-EATING BACTERIA

Flesh-eating bacteria don't exactly eat skin, though it sure seems like they do. These bacteria can get inside a person's body through a cut in

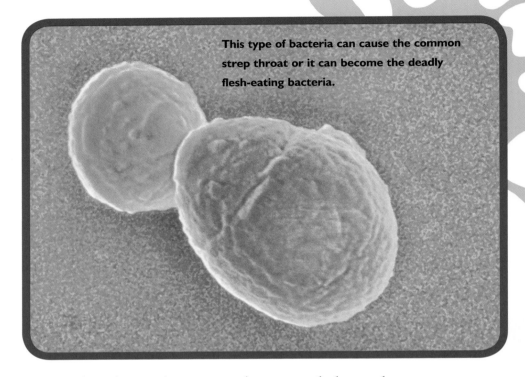

This type of bacteria can cause the common strep throat or it can become the deadly flesh-eating bacteria.

the skin. They may also spread through sneezing or coughing. When the bacteria get into the body, they release poisons. These poisons damage the tissues under the skin. Soon the skin and muscles will start to rot away.

Most infections with flesh-eating bacteria are caused by the same group of bacteria that cause common strep throat. At first, the infected patch of skin looks red and swollen and feels hot. The skin really hurts. Most cases of flesh-eating bacteria are mild and can be treated with medicine if caught early. But sometimes fluid-filled blisters may appear, and the skin turns bluish gray.

As nerves in the skin are destroyed, the area becomes numb. Flesh-eating bacteria infections may get so bad that the person loses all feeling in a finger, a toe, or even an arm or a leg. The infected body part may have to be amputated (surgically cut off) to keep the disease from spreading.

Yikes! A flesh-eating bacteria infection spreads very quickly. It can start out as small as a pimple and spread to an entire leg in less than half an hour!

CHAPTER THREE

Was It Something I Ate?

WORM INVADERS

Do you like to eat your hamburger a little rare? That may not be a good idea. Sometimes undercooked beef and especially pork may contain live tapeworm eggs! How did they get there? Cows and pigs may swallow tapeworm eggs when they eat unclean food. The eggs hatch inside their intestines. The young tapeworms make their way through the bloodstream and then to the muscles. The meat people eat is mostly muscles. Tapeworms can spread to people when infected animals are killed for food.

A tapeworm is ribbon-shaped—long and flat. (That's how it got its name.) Its head has little hooks that cling to the inside of the intestines.

Yikes! An adult tapeworm may grow up to fifteen meters (fifty feet) long! Even at that length it can fit inside a person's body because it is so thin and flat.

What Goes Around . . .

How do tapeworm eggs get into soil and animal food? In some countries, people's body wastes are dumped into rivers and streams. They may even be used as fertilizer for crops. So if the people had tapeworms, the worm eggs can end up in soil, grass, and water.

The rest of its body is made up of hundreds of segments. The segments break off easily and pass out in poop. Each segment contains thousands of eggs. A single adult tapeworm can produce more than a million eggs a day!

It's pretty gross to imagine having worms—or even their eggs—inside your body! Sometimes people don't realize that they have tapeworms unless they see them in their poop. But others may feel sick to their stomach, have diarrhea, and lose weight. Worms may even get into the brain and cause mental problems. Luckily, doctors have medicines that can kill tapeworms.

GOING "MAD"

When mad cow disease made news headlines, people panicked. "Don't eat hamburgers!" some said. Health officials warned the public that the meat could cause a terrifying disease. Even though this disease is extremely rare in humans, many people were afraid to eat meat.

Mad cow disease is caused by harmful proteins called prions. They are found in the brain tissue of infected cattle. Prions eat holes into the brain, leaving it looking like a sponge. The animals are literally losing their minds. The disease got its name because the infected cattle stagger around and act weird. Eventually, they die.

Until 1997 farmers used cattle feed containing animal parts (including bits of brain tissue) to help their cows grow faster. That's how mad cow disease spread.

Cooking does not destroy prions. So if

Yikes! Mad cow disease can take a long time for symptoms to develop—up to ten years! Meanwhile, cows could be infected and no one would know it.

people eat meat from infected cattle, they may develop the human form of mad cow disease. Symptoms may include memory loss, mood changes, dizziness, difficulty walking, muscle spasms, loss of speech, and blindness. Scientists have not yet found a cure.

The first human case of mad cow disease was reported in Great Britain in 1994. However, as of mid-2008, fewer than two hundred people in the world had died of mad cow disease—and only one person in the United States.

Body Bugs

CREEPY CRAWLIES

Imagine tiny little bugs crawling underneath your skin, eating your skin cells, and then laying eggs there. Soon you develop a really itchy rash on your skin—just above the place where the little critters made their home. Sound creepy? That's what happens when someone has scabies.

Scabies is a skin rash caused by mites. Mites are related to spiders. They are extremely tiny and very hard to see. An adult mite is about the size of a pinhead. People can get scabies when they have a lot of close contact with someone who has it. Mites can spread easily in crowded places, such as day care centers, classrooms, and college dorms. If there is skin-to-skin contact, the tiny mites can move from one person to another. They may also spread to a person who uses a towel, clothing, or sheets recently used by someone with scabies.

Once the scabies mites have found a new home, the females start to dig tunnels beneath the top layer of the person's skin. They lay eggs there and die about a month later. Soon the eggs hatch.

Yikes! You probably have mites living all over you right now! There are eyelash mites, eyebrow mites, face mites, and mites on other parts of the body. You don't realize they are there because they are very tiny— microscopic. They just live quietly, feeding on dead skin cells, and don't cause any trouble.

This eyelash mite was magnified with a microscope.

Once the new mites grow up, they come to the skin surface. Males and females find each other and mate. The males die, and the females dig back down beneath the skin surface and lay new eggs.

Meanwhile, the person's body may react to the mites' new living arrangements. Soon a dry, itchy, reddish rash of bumps appears. Often these bumps may form thin lines on the skin where the mites have been digging. The rash is especially common on the wrists and between the fingers. Scratching can cause a scabies infection, which may produce pus-filled bumps. Luckily, scabies is easy to treat.

NIT PICKING

What are those tiny white dots in your hair? And why has your scalp been itching so much? Just a bad case of dandruff? Oh, no! You've got head lice!

Lice are tiny insects, about the size of sesame seeds. They live on animals' skin, hiding out among the hairs. Head lice live on people's heads. They stick their needle-sharp mouthparts into the scalp and suck up blood. There are also body lice that live on other hairy parts of the human body.

Yikes! Monkeys and apes get lice, too. They spend a lot of time grooming each other, picking off lice and nits (eggs). They don't throw the lice away—they eat them!

You can't just brush off head lice. Their six legs end in hooklike claws that cling tightly to the hairs. They can hang on even if you go swimming! A female louse lays about six tiny eggs (called nits) each day. The nits won't fall off by themselves because she glues each one to the base of a hair. Unless someone picks them off, or combs them out with a fine-tooth comb, the nits stay glued to the hairs for one or two weeks, until they hatch.

Head lice are found mainly on preschoolers, young schoolchildren, and their family members. They usually spread by head-to-head contact.

Body lice spread by contact and also by touching dirty clothes or bedding. They are mostly found among people who don't wash or change their clothes very often.

Body lice can spread some serious diseases. But head lice are just an itchy, crawly nuisance. Fortunately, there are medicated shampoos, soaps, and lotions that kill lice. Washing clothes, bedding, and hairbrushes in hot water can keep lice from coming back.

CHAPTER FIVE

Skin Deep

ELEPHANT LEGS

No one wants to be told they have elephant legs.
But some people *do* develop thick, baggy skin like
the skin on the legs of elephants. They have a
rare condition called elephantiasis. This causes
a person's legs or other body parts to swell up
to three times their normal size! The condition
may become so severe that people with it cannot
move around at all.

Elephantiasis is caused by microscopic,
threadlike worms. Infected mosquitoes transfer
them to people when they bite. The worms enter
a person's blood and then live and multiply in
the lymph vessels. (These are tubes that carry
fluids from the tissues back to the heart.) As the

Elephantiasis causes parts of the body to swell, often the legs and feet.

worms multiply, they may block some of the lymph vessels. Fluids then build up in the tissues. Some parts of the body, often the legs and feet, swell up like water balloons.

There are treatments for elephantiasis. They include drugs that kill the worms. Researchers are also working on vaccines to prevent the disease.

Yikes! The worst case of elephantiasis was seen in an Egyptian woman. Her leg was so swollen that it weighed 59 kilograms (130 pounds)! That was more than the weight of the rest of her body.

GRUESOME GANGRENE

A bad case of gangrene can make a person's fingers or toes fall off! Now that's pretty gross! How is that even possible? Gangrene develops when an injury or a disease destroys the tissues in part of the body, usually the hands or feet. Cells and tissues are kept alive by oxygen and other important nutrients in the blood. Tissues die when their blood supply is blocked or stopped. Eventually, the skin and dead tissue turn black and shrink. If the condition is not treated quickly, the affected body part—such as a finger or a toe—can actually fall off.

Gangrene may develop when an injury cuts blood vessels supplying an area. Wounds may also lead to gangrene when they get infected with bacteria. The infection causes a lot of swelling, which blocks off the blood supply to that part of the body. Eventually, the tissue dies. Frostbite can sometimes lead to gangrene, too. The area becomes so cold that the blood cannot flow properly.

Gangrene caused by bacteria can spread to other parts of the body. If it is not treated early enough, doctors may have to remove the affected area to stop it from spreading.

Yikes! Brown recluse spider bites can cause a circular area of gangrene around the bite. That's because the venom (poison) destroys the blood vessels and blocks the flow of blood.

CHAPTER SIX

A Fungus Is Among Us

ATHLETE'S FOOT

You don't have to be an athlete to get athlete's foot. But many athletes *do* get it—which is how it got its name. Athlete's foot is caused by a fungus that feeds on dead skin cells of the feet.

A fungus is a plantlike organism that doesn't need sunlight to survive. In fact, it grows best in warm, dark, damp environments. Fungi can be found in places where athletes hang out—around pools, public showers, and locker rooms. If you walk barefoot in these areas, some of the fungi living there might wind up on your feet. That's why it's a good idea to wear flip-flops or other shoes at community pools or public showers.

Fungi can thrive on the bottoms of a person's feet, especially inside hot and sweaty sneakers. The conditions there are dark, warm, and moist— perfect for fungi to grow and multiply. Eventually, the skin on the soles of the feet becomes red, cracked, and scaly, especially between the toes.

People can help prevent athlete's foot by keeping their feet dry after swimming, showering, or bathing. Using powder on the feet, wearing clean socks (even with sneakers or sandals), and changing shoes if they are damp may help, too.

NAIL FUNGUS

When a toenail or a fingernail turns yellowish and gets bumpy and yucky looking, it could be infected with nail fungus. This isn't the same as athlete's foot, which affects the skin of the feet. It is usually caused by a different kind of fungus, which feeds on the protein in the nails. This important protein keeps nails hard and healthy.

Nail fungus is more likely to occur in toenails than fingernails. That's because toenails spend a lot of time inside your shoes, where it's dark,

Ringworm

Ringworm is not really caused by worms. It is actually a fungus infection of the skin, like athlete's foot. Its name comes from the fact that the red rash it causes is often ring-shaped, with healthy-looking skin in the middle.

warm, and moist. Fingernails don't usually stay moist very long—the air dries them out.

A nail fungus infection may start out as a white or yellow spot under the tip of a toenail or a fingernail. As the fungus spreads deeper into the nail, the nail may change color. The nail starts to thicken and get crumbly at the edges. Unfortunately, nail fungus is very difficult to treat. You have to take medication for up to six months to get rid of the nail fungus. Sometimes the toenail has to be removed!

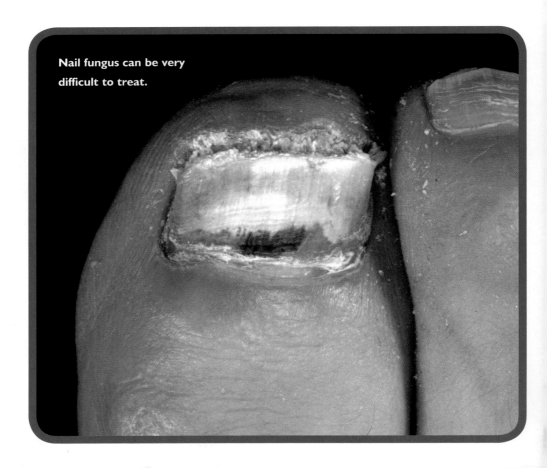

Nail fungus can be very difficult to treat.

Scary Skeletons

THE HUNCHBACK OF NOTRE DAME

Have you ever heard of Quasimodo, the main character in the story *The Hunchback of Notre Dame?* He was a bell-ringer who lived in the bell tower in Notre Dame. He had a huge, hunched-over back. His was an extreme case. It was so gruesome that many people were afraid of him. They taunted and teased him.

While the hunchback of Notre Dame was a made-up character, he actually had a real-life medical condition. Hunchback occurs when the upper part of the spine (backbone) bulges outward, causing a person to hunch over. In extreme cases, this condition can cause lung and heart problems because it reduces the amount of space for the organs inside the body.

A mild form of hunchback may develop due to poor posture—slouching over while standing or sitting. Doing back-strengthening exercises in front of a mirror may be all that is needed to correct this problem.

In other cases, the bones of the spine may not be shaped properly from birth, or some of the back muscles may be weak. These conditions may be hereditary or due to an injury or a disease. Treatments include physical therapy, wearing a brace, and surgery to straighten the spine.

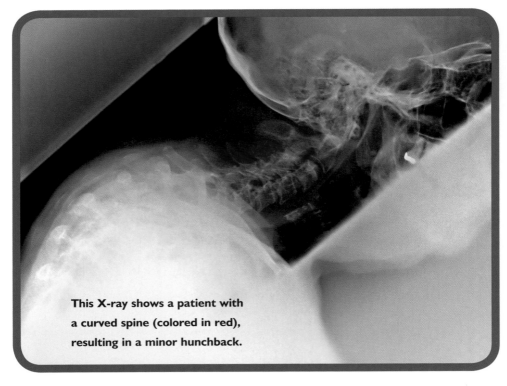

This X-ray shows a patient with a curved spine (colored in red), resulting in a minor hunchback.

Got Curves?

Everybody's spine is curved somewhat. In fact, the human spine, viewed from the side, looks like an S-shaped curve. The upper part of the spine curves toward the back, and the lower part curves toward the belly. In someone with a hunchback the upper spine is curved more than usual. It may also be twisted to the side, so that the hump seems to be above one shoulder.

STONE MAN SYNDROME

Running, jumping, catching and throwing a ball, combing your hair, changing your clothes, sitting down, writing your name . . . . Practically everything you do involves moving some part of your body. An inner skeleton of bones, along with muscles that pull on the bones, helps you move. But for a few thousand people in the world,

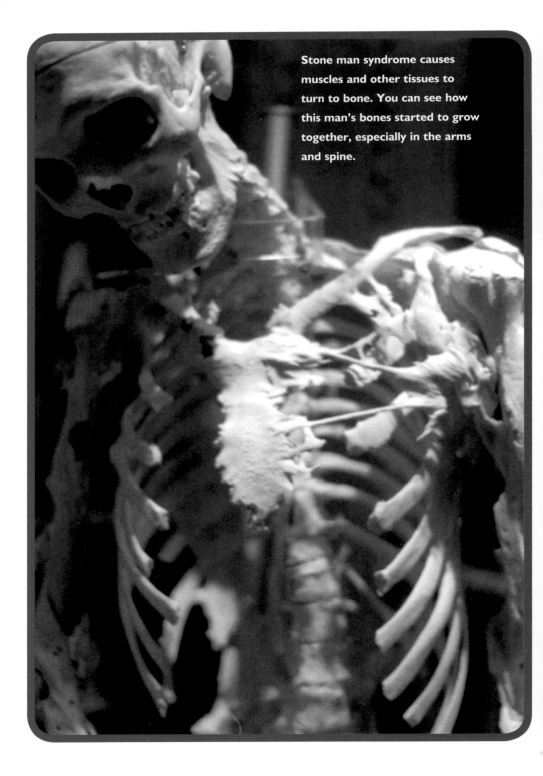

Stone man syndrome causes muscles and other tissues to turn to bone. You can see how this man's bones started to grow together, especially in the arms and spine.

everyday movements get more and more difficult. They have inherited a serious condition that is caused by a very rare gene. (A gene is a chemical that determines people's traits, such as eye color or height.)

This condition is called stone man syndrome. Muscles and other soft tissues turn into bone. A minor bump or bruise can cause a new lump of bone to form. It grows rapidly and may join with bones of the skeleton, locking the joints so they can't move. The process usually starts at the neck and moves downward—to the shoulders, arms, chest, and finally the legs and feet. Eventually, patients may not be able to move at all.

Doctors do not yet have a cure for stone man syndrome. But in 2006, researchers discovered the gene that causes it. This gene helps to form the skeleton of a developing baby. Normally, this gene stops working soon after birth. But about one in 2 million people inherit a faulty gene that keeps on working. Now that researchers know what causes stone man syndrome, they are looking for ways to fix the faulty gene.

CHAPTER
EIGHT

Monster Conditions

THE ELEPHANT MAN

In the 1800s, Joseph Merrick was considered a freak show. He had a health condition that caused frightening changes in his head and body. Merrick was so scary looking that people called him the Elephant Man.

When Merrick was born, he seemed perfectly healthy. But at age two, his body started to go through some unusual changes. Strange, dark growths appeared on his skin. Then lumps started to develop under his skin, on his neck, on his chest, and on the back of his head. Kids in the neighborhood laughed at him.

Later, a big bulge formed on the right side of Merrick's head. His right arm and hand grew much larger than his left. When he was twelve years old, Merrick's right hand was so deformed that he couldn't use it. By his teen years, the growths on his skin were huge.

Joseph Merrick, the "Elephant Man," suffered from a rare disease that made parts of his body grow much larger than usual.

Yikes! When Joseph Merrick was an adult, his head measured one meter (three feet) around. It was so large and heavy that he had to sleep sitting up. But one morning in 1890 Merrick was found lying in bed on his back. He was dead. His head was so heavy that it had crushed his windpipe. He was only twenty-eight years old.

At first, doctors thought Joseph Merrick had elephantiasis. But medical experts now realize that he had a severe form of a very rare hereditary disease known as elephant man disease. The condition is caused by a faulty gene that causes the head and feet to grow to giant size. Sometimes one side of the body grows much larger than the other. Surgery can help this condition these days.

REAL-LIFE WEREWOLVES

You've heard the werewolf legends: On the night of a full moon, a man transforms into a mythical beast—a werewolf. He grows a furry coat and long fangs and has superhuman strength.

We all love a good werewolf story. But what if they were real? A medical condition called werewolf syndrome actually exists! This is a genetic condition that causes people to grow long, thick hair covering most of their body. These people look a lot like werewolves—but they don't get the fangs and the cool powers.

Werewolf syndrome is a very rare genetic condition. It affects only two or three families in the world. In one family, about twenty members (both men and women) have the condition. Even those who do not have the disease may carry the gene for it and then pass it on to their children.

People with werewolf syndrome are often teased or tormented. In the past, these people were often kept in cages, and viewers paid a fee to see them. But these days, some people with the condition choose to use their appearance to make a living and entertain people. Danny Gomez and his older brother, Larry, for example, are acrobats in a Mexican circus.

Do Vampires Exist?

If there are real-life werewolves, could there be real vampires, too? Not exactly. There's a medical condition, though, that might make people *seem* like vampires. Their skin is sensitive to sunlight. When they go out in the sun, they may quickly get sunburned and develop blisters or scars. It can be very painful. These real-life vampires may also need extra blood. But they get it from blood transfusions, not by biting people!

They don't mind being called wolf men. They just enjoy performing daredevil tricks and traveling with the circus.

There is no treatment for werewolf syndrome. Some people just accept the way they were born. Others try to remove the extra hair.

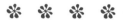

The diseases in this book are yucky and often scary, too. Fortunately, most of them are very rare. There are now cures for some of them, and medical researchers are working to learn more and find effective treatments and cures for the others.

WORDS TO KNOW

bacteria—Single-celled microscopic organisms, some of which cause diseases.

buboe—A swollen lymph gland.

bubonic plague—A disease caused by a bacterium, named for its typical symptom: buboes.

Ebola—A disease caused by a deadly virus that results in high fever and internal bleeding.

elephantiasis—A condition caused by threadlike worms living inside the body.

gangrene—Death and rotting of body tissues as a result of lack of blood to an area.

gene—A chemical that carries hereditary information determining a particular trait of an organism.

inherited—Passed on by genes from parents to children; also called hereditary or genetic.

leprosy—A disease that affects the skin and nerves, causing sores on the skin and loss of feeling (numbness); a person with leprosy is called a leper.

prion—A defective protein known to cause diseases of the nervous system, such as the human form of mad cow disease.

scabies—A skin condition caused by mites that burrow underneath the skin, where they lay eggs.

FURTHER READING

Books

Branzei, Sylvia. *Hands-On Grossology*. New York: Price Stern Sloan, 2003.

Claybourne, Anna. *The Usborne Complete Book of the Human Body*. London: Usborne Publishing Ltd., 2006.

Rosenberg, Pam. *Eew! Icky, Sticky, Gross Stuff in Your Body*. Child's World, 2007.

Szpirglas, Jeff. *Gross Universe: Your Guide to All Disgusting Things Under the Sun*. Toronto, Ontario: Maple Tree Press, Inc., 2004.

Internet Addresses

Centers for Disease Control and Prevention (CDC). "BAM! Body and Mind."

<http://www.bam.gov/>

A fun site about diseases, nutrition, safety, and your body. Includes information about "The Immune Platoon" that defends your body against disease, how the CDC detects infection, and features on SARS and West Nile virus.

Kids Health. "What's Mad Cow Disease?"

<http://kidshealth.org/kid/talk/qa/mad_cow_disease.html>

Simple information about what mad cow disease is and how you get it, what's being done about it, and what you can do.

Index